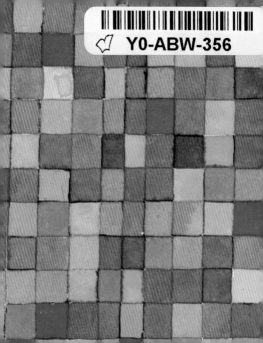

The Gift of
Friendship

THE GIFT OF

Friendship

Edited by Margaret Lannamann

Illustrated by Anne Smith

Ariel Books

**Andrews McMeel
Publishing**

Kansas City

www.andrewsmcmeel.com

ISBN: 0-8362-6809-1
Library of Congress Catalog Card Number:
98-84239

Contents

Introduction

How can we ever say enough about how important friends are to us? Friends share in our day-to-day lives, in our joys and sorrows. Friends laugh at our jokes and cheer us up when we're down. Friends offer love and comfort when we need it—and even when we don't.

The affection and loyalty of friends make our days immeasurably richer. Anything life brings our way becomes more meaningful when we experience it with a friend. The bond between us is constant and enduring; the joys we share together are some of life's greatest blessings.

A
Definition of
Friendship

Friendship is one heart in
two bodies.
—Joseph Zabara

My friends are my estate.
—Emily Dickinson

A true friend is the best
possession.
—Benjamin Franklin

On the road between
the homes of friends,

grass does not grow.

—Norwegian proverb

Friendship is a
sheltering tree.

—Samuel Taylor Coleridge

No person is your friend who
demands your silence, or denies
your right to grow.
—Alice Walker

Friendships are glued together
with little kindnesses.
—Mercia Tweedale

You said just the thing that I
wished you to say. And you made
me believe that you meant it.

—Grace Stricker Dawson

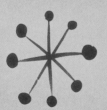

You cannot be friends
upon any other terms than
upon the terms of equality.

—Woodrow Wilson

Friendship is Love
without his wings!

—Lord Byron

FRIENDSHIP:
1 part
commonality
1 part
difference
Mix
thoroughly...

One recipe for friendship
is the right mixture of
commonality and difference.
You've got to have enough in
common so that you under-
stand each other and enough
difference so that there is
something to exchange.

—Robert Weiss

Friends Old and New

The growth of true friendship
may be a lifelong affair.
—Sarah Orne Jewett

Think where man's glory most
begins and ends
And say my glory was I had
such friends.
—William Butler Yeats

Two may talk together under the same roof for many years, yet never really meet; and two others at first speech are old friends.

—Mary Catherwood

Old friends, like old
wines, don't lose
their flavor.

—Jewish proverb

A friend may well
be reckoned the
masterpiece of nature.

—Ralph Waldo Emerson

Familiarity breeds content.
—Anna Quindlen

You can make more friends in
two months by becoming more
interested in other people than
you can in two years by trying to
get people interested in you.
—Dale Carnegie

I felt it shelter to speak to you.
—Emily Dickinson

true friend

Hold a true friend with
both your hands.

—Nigerian proverb

You can date the evolving
life of the mind, like the
age of a tree, by the rings

of friendship formed
by the expanding
central trunk.

—Mary McCarthy

Are we not like the two
volumes of one book?

—Marceline Desbordes-Valmore

Shared
Laughter

A friend is one who knows all about you and likes you anyway.
—Christi Mary Warner

No people feel closer or more friendly than those who are on the same diet.
—Anonymous

You can always tell a real friend:
When you've made a fool of
yourself he doesn't feel you've
done a permanent job.
—Laurence J. Peter

A good friend—like a
tube of toothpaste—
comes through in a tight
squeeze.

—Anonymous

tooth-
paste

Wear a smile and have friends; wear a scowl and have wrinkles.

—George Eliot

You can keep your
friends by not giving
them away.

—Mary Pettibone Poole

Friendship is not possible
between two women
one of whom is very
well dressed.

—Laurie Colwin

I don't like to commit
myself about heaven and
hell—

you see, I have friends in

both places.

—Mark Twain

Good Times
and Bad

Show me a friend who will weep
with me; those who will laugh
with me I can find myself.
—Slavic proverb

True friendship is never serene.
—Marie de Sévigné

The problems that plague a friendship are rarely 100 percent the other person's fault. We should self-examine carefully before we make up our mind—and before we close it.

—Judith Viorst

It is the friends that

you can

A.M.

call at 4 A.M. that matter.

—Marlene Dietrich

I can trust my friends. . . . These people force me to examine myself, encourage me to grow.
—Cher

I have no trouble with my enemies. But my goddam friends . . . they are the ones that keep me walking the floor nights.
—Warren G. Harding

The only way to have a friend
is to be one.
—Ralph Waldo Emerson

Every man should have a
fair-sized cemetery in
which to bury the faults
of his friends.

—Henry Brooks Adams

Friendship is like money,
easier made than kept.

—Samuel Butler

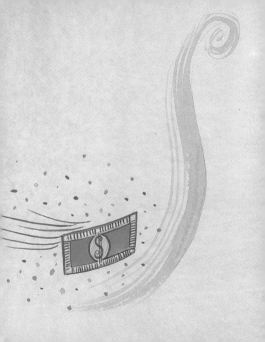

What do we live for, if it is
not to make life less difficult
for each other?
—George Eliot

Sooner or later you've heard all
your best friends have to say. Then
comes the tolerance of real love.
—Ned Rorem

The easiest kind of relationship
for me is with ten thousand
people. The hardest is with one.
—Joan Baez

The only thing to do is to
hug one's friends tight and
do one's job.
—Edith Wharton

A friend is someone who
understands your past,
believes in your future,
and accepts you today just
the way you are.

—Proverbs 27:17

Friends
Together

Sticks in a bundle are
unbreakable.

—Kenyan proverb

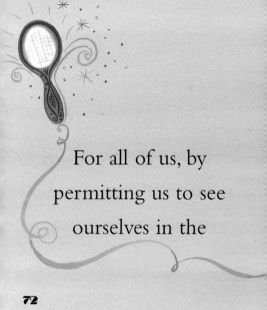

For all of us, by

permitting us to see

ourselves in the

mirror of their affection,
friends help to anchor
our self-image, to validate
our identity.

—Lillian B. Rubin

Reinforce the stitch that ties us, and I will do the same for you.

—Doris Schwerin

Two people holding each other
up like flying buttresses. Two
people depending on each other
and babying each other and
defending each other against the
world outside.

—Erica Jong

There are three things that grow
more precious with age; old wood
to burn, old books to read, and
old friends to enjoy.
—Henry Ford

To love is to make
of one's heart a
swinging door.

—Howard Thurman

This book was

designed and typeset

by Junie Lee

in New York City.